The
Chimpanzee

Published by Raintree Steck-Vaughn Publishers, an imprint of Steck-Vaughn Company.

Acknowledgments
Project Editor: Helene Resky
Design Manager: Joyce Spicer
Consulting Editor: Kim Merlino
Consultant: Michael Chinery
Illustrated by Robert Morton
Designed by Ian Winton and Steve Prosser
Electronic Cover Production: Alan Klemp
Additional Electronic Production: Bo McKinney and Scott Melcer
Photography credits on page 32

Planned and produced by The Creative Publishing Company

Library of Congress Cataloging-in-Publication Data
    Crewe, Sabrina
    The chimpanzee / Sabrina Crewe ; [illustrated by Robert Morton].
        p.   cm. — (Life cycles)
    Includes index.
    Summary: Describes the habitat, eating habits, and life cycle of the chimpanzee.
    ISBN 0-8172-4368-2 (hardcover). — ISBN 0-8172-6231-8 (pbk.)
    1. Chimpanzees — Juvenile literature.   2. Chimpanzees — Life cycles — Juvenile
literature. [1. Chimpanzees.]   I. Morton, Robert.   II. Title.   III. Series: Crewe, Sabrina.
Life cycles.
QL737.P96C74   1997
599.88'44 — dc20   96-4826
                                                                            CIP   AC

        3 4 5 6 7 8 9 LB 03 02
Printed and bound in the United States of America.

Words explained in the glossary appear in
bold the first time they are used in the text.

LIFE CYCLES

The
Chimpanzee

Sabrina Crewe

RSVP
RAINTREE
STECK-VAUGHN
PUBLISHERS
The Steck-Vaughn Company

The chimpanzee has a new baby.

The baby chimpanzee is a few weeks old. It drinks milk from its mother. The mother keeps the baby next to her all the time.

The baby holds on tight.

The mother chimpanzee doesn't need to hold the baby to keep it close. The baby can hold onto its mother's fur. When it gets bigger, the baby will ride on its mother's back.

The baby is learning to climb.

The baby chimpanzee has long
fingers and toes. It uses them
to hold onto the branch while
it climbs. Chimpanzees spend
more time in trees than they do
on the ground.

Chimpanzees live in groups.

Chimpanzees like to be with other
chimpanzees. Sometimes they live in
a big group. Mother chimpanzees may
make a small group with other mothers
while their babies are very young.

The chimpanzee wants to play!

The young chimpanzee is one year old.
It bounces up and down on the branch.
It wants to play a game with the other
chimpanzees in its group.

The chimpanzee swings through the forest.

The young chimpanzee is learning to move quickly through the trees. It pulls itself from branch to branch and swings on **vines**. Chimpanzees can travel through trees without ever touching the ground.

It is raining.

When the wet season starts, it rains every day. The chimpanzees don't like the rain. They come close together and stay still.

After it rains, new plants start to
grow. There will be more food for
the chimpanzees.

The chimpanzee has found some food.

Male chimpanzees hoot and scream when they find food. They are calling the mothers and young chimpanzees to share the food. The young chimpanzees soon learn what is good to eat.

The young chimpanzee finds its own food.

The chimpanzee is three years old. It has learned to look for food in the trees. Chimpanzees find nuts, berries, and other fruit. Sometimes they eat green shoots, insects, and other small animals.

The termites taste good.

The chimpanzee has found a log full of
termites. It puts a stick into the log and
pulls it out again. The stick is covered
with termites for the chimpanzee to eat.

The chimpanzee is cracking a nut.

The young chimpanzee has learned to crack nuts. The chimpanzee puts the nut on a stone. Then it bangs the nut hard with another stone until it cracks.

Night is coming.

It is time to make a bed for the night.
Chimpanzees spend their nights in trees.
This keeps them safe while they sleep.

The young chimpanzee makes
its own bed next to its mother.
It bends the leafy branches of
the tree to form a nest.

Chimpanzees are travelers.

Chimpanzees don't stay in the same place every night. They travel around with other chimpanzees in their group. They share their **home range** with many chimpanzees from the same place.

The chimpanzee is growing up.

The young chimpanzee spends less time with his mother. He likes to be with older males and copy what they do. They let him join in for a while.

The chimpanzee is by himself.

The chimpanzee is seven years old.
He has left his mother. He stays in
his home range, but he moves from
one group to another.

The chimpanzee makes a challenge.

When male chimpanzees grow up,
they start to **challenge** group leaders.
They make noisy **displays**, so they
seem bigger than they really are.

The chimpanzees are excited.

The chimpanzees have met another group from their home range. They shake branches, jump up and down, and call to each other. Some of them may join the other group for a while.

The chimpanzees are grooming each other.

The chimpanzees are pleased to see each other. **Grooming** helps chimpanzees to get along. It makes them feel calm and safe.

The chimpanzee has found a mate.

A young female may leave her mother's group when she is eight or nine years old. She will mate with a male from another group. Her baby will be born seven months later.

Chimpanzees live out of the wild.

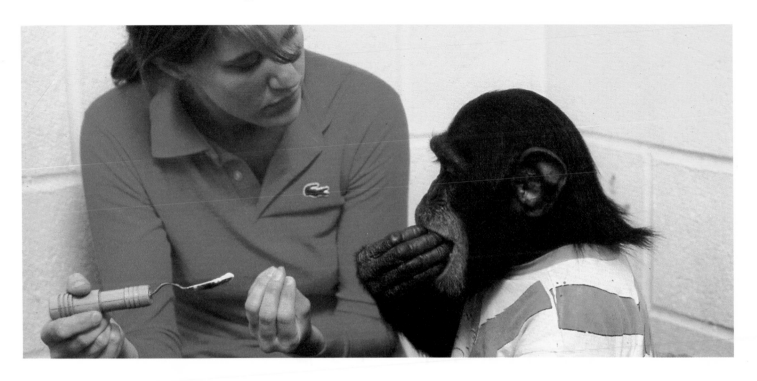

Many chimpanzees have been brought to live with people who want to find out more about them. People have taught chimpanzees to understand words and to figure out the answers to problems.

This chimpanzee is learning to talk with people by using sign language. The chimpanzee is being shown a sign for the word *eat*.

Chimpanzees need forests.

Chimpanzees need plenty of space. They need trees where they can find food and make nests. People can help chimpanzees by saving their forests. They can also keep chimpanzees from being captured and taken to zoos and **laboratories**.

Chimpanzees are apes.

Apes are the group of animals most like people. They have long arms, no tails, and live in trees as well as on the ground. Apes and monkeys belong to a group of **mammals** called **primates**. You can tell monkeys from apes, because monkeys do have tails. Here are some other apes and monkeys.

APES

Gibbon

Gorilla

Orangutan

Marmoset

Colobus
monkey

MONKEYS

Spider monkey

Rhesus
monkey

29

Where the Chimpanzee Lives

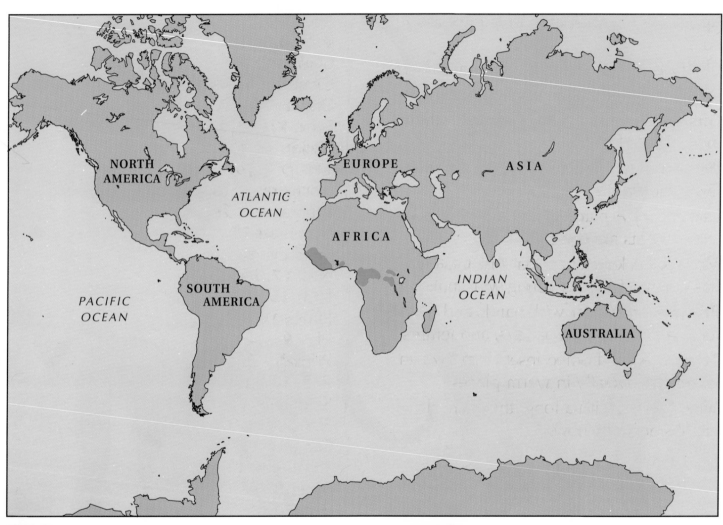

 Areas where the chimpanzee lives

Glossary

Ape A furry animal with long arms and no tail

Challenge To dare another animal to fight

Display To make a show of something

Groom To clean the fur of another animal by picking at it

Home range The area in which an animal lives and travels

Laboratory A place where scientific experiments are done

Mammal A kind of animal that usually has fur and feeds its young with milk

Primate An animal with hands and feet, such as apes, monkeys, and lemurs

Termite A soft-bodied insect that lives in groups, especially in warm places

Vine A plant with a long, thin stem that climbs or hangs down

Index

Photography credits

Front cover: (top left) Rod Williams/Bruce Coleman; (middle left) Clive Bromhall/Oxford Scientific Films; (bottom left) Peter Dewey/Bruce Coleman; (right) Clive Bromhall/Oxford Scientific Films.

Title page: Peter Jackson/Bruce Coleman; p. 4: Karl Ammann; p. 5: Zig Leszczynski/Animals Animals/Oxford Scientific Films; p. 6: Tom McHugh/PhotoResearchers/Oxford Scientific Films; p. 7: Konrad Wothe/Oxford Scientific Films; p. 8: Mike Birkhead/Oxford Scientific Films; p. 9: Peter Jackson/Bruce Coleman; p. 10: John Mackinnon/Bruce Coleman; p. 12: Andrew Plumptre/Oxford Scientific Films; p. 13: Michael W. Richards/Oxford Scientific Films; p. 14: Peter Davey/Bruce Coleman; p. 15: Neil Bromhall/Oxford Scientific Films; p. 17: Dieter and Mary Plage/Bruce Coleman; p. 18: Clive Bromhall/Oxford Scientific Films; p. 19: Karl Ammann; p. 20: Silvestris/FLPA; p. 21: Clive Bromhall/Oxford Scientific Films; p. 23: Steve Turner/Oxford Scientific Films; p. 24: Karl Ammann; p. 25: H. S. Terrace/Animals Animals/Oxford Scientific Films; p. 27: Michael W. Richards/Oxford Scientific Films.